GREAT AFRICAN AMERICANS IN
SPORTS

PAT REDIGER

Crabtree Publishing Company

Dedication

This series is dedicated to the African-American men and women who dared to follow their dreams. With courage, faith, and hard work, they overcame obstacles in their lives and went on to excel in their fields. They fought for civil rights and encouraged hope and self-reliance. They celebrated the glory of the athlete and the joy of knowledge and learning. They brought entertainment, poetry, and song to the world, and we are richer for it. *Outstanding African Americans* is both an acknowledgement of and a tribute to these people.

Project Manager
Amanda Woodrow

Writing Team
Karen Dudley
Pat Rediger

Editor
Virginia Mainprize

Research
Karen Dudley

Design and layout
Warren Clark
Karen Dudley

Photograph Credits

Archive Photos: pages 13, 44, 49 (Popperfoto), 52 (Shen); **Reuters/Bettman:** pages 21, 24, 29, 38; **UPI/Bettman:** pages 6, 31, 43, 55, 61; **Blackstar:** pages 4 (Johnston), 5, 9 (Schulke), 10 (Barns), 18 (Bakke), 28 (Marzullo); **Canapress Photo Service:** pages 14, 17, 30, 32, 33; **Globe Photos:** pages 7, 8, 11, 15, 22, 40, 41, 42, 45, 46, 58; **Ponopresse Internationale Inc.:** pages 19, 20, 23, 25, 26, 27, 34, 37; **Retna Ltd.:** pages 12 (Seitz/Stills), 16 (Granitz), 39 (Siaud/Stills); **Urban Archives, Temple University:** pages 35, 36.

Published by
Crabtree Publishing Company

350 Fifth Avenue,	360 York Road, R.R. 4	73 Lime Walk
Suite 3308	Niagara-on-the-Lake,	Headington
New York, New York	Ontario Canada	Oxford Ox3 7AD
U.S.A. 10018	L0S 1J0	United Kingdom

Cataloging-in-Publication Data

Rediger, Pat, 1966-
    Great African Americans in sports/by Pat Rediger.
      p. cm. — (Outstanding African Americans series)
    Includes index.
    Summary: Profiles notable African Americans in the field of sports, including Muhammad Ali, Arthur Ashe, and Zina Garrison.
    ISBN 0-86505-801-6 (lib. bdg.) — ISBN 0-86505-815-6 (pbk.)
1. Afro-American athletes—Biography—Juvenile literature.
[1. Athletes. 2. Afro-Americans—Biography.] I. Title. II. Series. Rediger, Pat, 1966- Outstanding African Americans series.
    GV697.AIR43 1995   95-24880
    796'.092'2—dc20   CIP
    [B]   AC

Contents

Muhammad Ali

Personality Profile

Career: Boxer.

Born: January 17, 1942, in Louisville, Kentucky, to Cassius and Odessa Clay.

Family: Married Sonji Roi, (divorced, 1966); married Belinda Boyd, 1967, (divorced, 1977); married Veronica Porche, 1977, (divorced); married Yolanda Williams, 1986. Has nine children, Khaliah, Laila, Maryum, Miya, Rasheeda, Muhammad, Jr., Herbert, Jamillah, and Hanna.

Awards: National Golden Gloves titles, 1959-60; Olympic gold medal in boxing, 1960; world heavyweight champion, 1964-67, 1974-78, 1978-79.

Growing Up

During his spare time, Joe Martin, a white policeman, trained young boxers at the Columbia Gym in Louisville, Kentucky. In 1954, he began training a shy twelve-year-old named Cassius Clay, Jr. Cassius had a natural ability to box. He had taken up the sport because in those days boxing was one of the few chances African Americans had for success. At the gym, Cassius met trainer Fred Stoner who taught him the art of boxing and the skill of moving lightly and quickly that would make him a champion. By the time he was eighteen, Cassius had won an Olympic gold medal and had become a professional boxer.

Even though he still ranked number nine, Cassius boasted that he would become the heavyweight champion of the world. His name began appearing in newspapers across the country. The more he talked, the more interest people showed in him.

But Cassius could do more than talk. After winning several matches, he finally got a chance to fight the world heavyweight boxing champion, Sonny Liston. It was an exciting showdown. Sonny was one of the hardest hitters in the ring, but Cassius was known for his skill and courage. Cassius told everyone that he could "float like a butterfly and sting like a bee." He won the fight and, in 1964, at the age of twenty-two, became the world's heavyweight boxing champion.

"I was only about eleven or twelve years old when I said, 'I'm gonna get famous so I can help my people.'"

Developing Skills

Muhammad trained hard for all of his matches. His training regime included skipping.

Just before his fight with Sonny, Cassius became interested in the civil rights movement. He was inspired by black activist Malcolm X and converted to the Muslim faith. He changed his name to Muhammad Ali.

Muhammad kept his title of world heavyweight champion when he fought Sonny again in 1965. In this fight, Muhammad knocked Sonny out in the first round. Muhammad continued to defend his title for the next two years. His powerful punches and light footwork won him nine matches in a row. Fans flocked to see him, and he became a boxing legend.

In 1967, Muhammad refused to fight in the Vietnam War, and he was stripped of his boxing title. However, he returned to the ring in November, 1970. He fought Jerry Quarry and won, regaining his title and reputation. In 1971, Muhammad fought Joe Frazier and lost. It was the first fight he had lost as a champion.

Muhammad and Joe fought a rematch in 1974, and this time Muhammad won. But he was still not heavyweight champion. He would have to beat George Foreman if he wanted to regain his title. George was younger and stronger, and most people expected Muhammad to lose the fight. But Muhammad used his speed to win the match in the eighth round.

Muhammad continued to defend his title for the next four years. He lost to Leon Spinks in 1978 but won the rematch later that year.

Toward the end of the 1970s, Muhammad seemed to be slowing down. In 1977, his doctor told him to retire. Muhammad refused to quit although by this time he was in his late thirties and old for a boxer. Two years later, he lost his title. In 1980, he lost a match to Larry Holmes, and a year later, he fought Trevor Berbick and lost. After sixty-one fights, Muhammad decided to retire.

Muhammad lost to Joe Frazier in their 1971 match, but won the 1974 rematch in the fourteenth round.

Accomplishments

1959 Won National Golden Gloves title.	**1974** Became heavyweight champion of the world for the third time.
1960 Won National Golden Gloves title, Olympic gold medal, and turned professional.	**1975** Co-wrote autobiography, *The Greatest — My Own Story*.
1963 Converted to the Muslim faith and changed his name to Muhammad Ali.	**1976** Starred in *The Greatest*, a movie about his life.
1964 Became heavyweight champion of the world.	**1978** Lost his title to Leon Spinks but regained it later in the year.
1965 Retained heavyweight champion title.	

Overcoming Obstacles

Winning the gold medal at the Olympic games in 1960 was a great triumph for eighteen-year-old Muhammad. He was so proud of his success that we wore his medal day and night. But winning the gold was not enough to overcome racial prejudice. One day, when Muhammad, wearing his medal, sat down at a counter of a restaurant in his own town, the waitress told him they did not serve blacks. Muhammad was furious and decided to fight for better conditions for African Americans. He joined the civil rights movement and converted to the Muslim religion.

One of the greatest challenges Muhammad faced happened when he refused to fight in the Vietnam War because of his Muslim beliefs. When he announced he would not go to Vietnam, politicians, the media, and many of his fans criticized him. The New York State Athletic Commission and the World Boxing Association took away his title and banned him from boxing in the United States.

Muhammad stuck by his beliefs. He told *Sports Illustrated* magazine, "I'm giving up my title, my wealth, maybe my future. Many great men have been tested for their religious beliefs. If I pass this test, I'll come out stronger than ever." Muhammad was sentenced to five years in prison for refusing to fight but was released, and his sentence was reversed.

During the late 1970s, Muhammad's movements began to slow down, but his doctors weren't quite sure what the problem was. After he retired from boxing, it was discovered that he had Parkinson's syndrome, a brain disease that causes muscle tremors. The doctors believed it was caused by the many hits to his head during his boxing career. Muhammad began to take medicine to keep the disease in check, and, for a time, he regained much of his energy. He is still affected by slurred speech and slower reflexes.

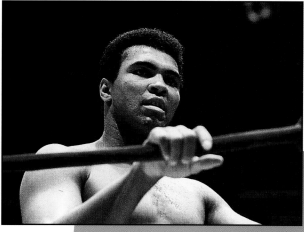

Muhammad training for a fight against Joe Frazier in 1970.

Although Muhammad earned millions of dollars as a professional boxer, much of it went to his managers. Today, Muhammad uses his time and money trying to help people, especially young African Americans. In 1990, he visited Our Children's Foundation, Inc. in Manhattan where he told the children, "The sun has a purpose. The moon has a purpose. The snow has a purpose. Cows have a purpose. You were born for a purpose. Go to school. Learn to read and write."

Special Interests

- In 1980, Muhammad worked as a supporter of President Jimmy Carter and the Democratic Party.
- In 1985, Muhammad and three advisers traveled to Lebanon where they unsuccessfully tried to gain the release of four kidnapped Americans. In 1990, he successfully bargained for the release of fourteen Americans who were being held hostage in Iran.

Arthur Ashe

Died: February 6, 1993, in New York, New York.

Family: Married Jeanne-Marie Moutoussamy, 1977. Had a daughter, Camera Elizabeth.

Education: University of California, Los Angeles (UCLA), B.A. in business administration, 1966.

Awards: Australian Open, 1970; French Open Doubles, 1972; World Champion Tennis Singles, 1975; Wimbledon Singles, 1975; Australian Open Doubles, 1977; elected to Tennis Hall of Fame, 1985; named *Sports Illustrated* Sportsman of the Year, 1992; Presidential Medal of Freedom, 1993.

Personality Profile

Career: Tennis player, writer, lecturer, tennis coach, and television commentator.

Born: July 10, 1943, in Richmond, Virginia, to Arthur, Sr. and Mattie Ashe.

Growing Up

Growing up in Richmond, Virginia, Arthur spent many hours at the playground. His father, Arthur, Sr., ran the largest park for blacks in the city, and the family lived in a cottage right on the grounds. Young Arthur was too small for football and too slow for track. One day, when he was seven, Arthur borrowed a racket and discovered tennis. His mother had just died, and Arthur practiced for hours to help him forget his loneliness.

A part-time playground instructor, Ronald Charity, noticed Arthur's talent. Because the city's tennis courts were segregated, and blacks and whites could not play together, Ronald realized Arthur would have to go somewhere else for special coaching. Ronald introduced Arthur to Dr. Walter Johnson, who coached and promoted black tennis players and gave them their equipment. Arthur spent several summers with Walter who taught him a lot about tennis including how to accept defeat and celebrate victory with good manners.

Arthur won many victories as an amateur tennis player before turning professional in 1969.

By the time he was fourteen, Arthur was a nationally ranked amateur tennis player. He won the National Junior Indoors Singles title in 1960 and 1961. His victories were noticed by Richard Hudlin, a tennis coach from St. Louis, Missouri. Richard asked Arthur if he would like to train with him while he finished high school in St. Louis. Arthur accepted. By 1962, when he was nineteen, he was the fifth-ranking junior player in the United States.

Developing Skills

I n 1962, Arthur accepted a scholarship to attend the University of California in Los Angeles (UCLA). Here, coach J.D. Morgan and tennis legend Pancho Gonzalez helped Arthur perfect his skills. In 1963, Arthur was named to the Davis Cup team, the first African American ever to be picked. He won a victory in his first national contest — the U.S. Men's Hard Court championship. Next year, Arthur was ranked as the sixth-best amateur player in America. He rose to second rank in 1965, after singles victories in the Davis Cup finals.

Arthur at a tennis tournament in France.

Arthur kept up his studies all during this time and graduated from university in June of 1966. He finished his college tennis career by leading UCLA to the National Collegiate Athletic Association (NCAA) championship. He won in both the singles and doubles competitions.

After graduating from UCLA, Arthur joined the U.S. Army. He served as a first lieutenant with the Reserve Officers' Training Corps. While he was with the army, he won the 1967 Men's Clay Court championship and the U.S. amateur title.

But the best was yet to come. Later in the year, he won the U.S. Open tournament. Arthur became the top-ranked American player in 1968. For the next six years, Arthur was among the top five tennis players in the world.

In 1969, Arthur turned professional and continued his rise to success. His best year was 1975, when he won both the Wimbledon Singles championship and the World Championship Tennis Singles. He was the first black man to win at Wimbledon and the first to receive a number-one ranking internationally. Many people considered him to be a pioneer because he had opened the way for black players in tennis.

In 1979, Arthur suffered a major heart attack and retired from the game. He became a spokesperson for minority athletes and worked as a television commentator at tennis matches, as well as consulting at tennis clinics. Arthur wrote *A Hard Road to Glory*, a three-volume history of black athletes in America. He also contributed a regular column for the *Washington Post*.

Arthur with the trophy he won at Wimbledon in 1975 when he won the men's singles title.

Accomplishments

1959 Became an amateur tennis player.	**1972** Won French Open Doubles.
1960-61 Won Junior Indoors Singles titles.	**1975** Won World Champion Tennis Singles and Wimbledon Singles.
1962 Became fifth-ranked junior player in the U.S.	**1977** Won Australian Open Doubles.
1963 Named to the Davis Cup team.	**1985** Elected to the Tennis Hall of Fame.
1965 Won singles competition in the Davis Cup finals and toured Australia.	**1988** Published *A Hard Road to Glory*.
1966 Led UCLA to the NCAA championship.	**1992** Named *Sports Illustrated* Sportsman of the Year.
1970 Won Australian Open.	

Overcoming Obstacles

Tennis was a difficult choice of career for Arthur because it was a game controlled by whites. Many times he suffered from racism. When he applied to play in tournaments, some white clubs said his application arrived "too late" and refused to let him enter the competition. When he did play, he was often the only black person on the court and was made to feel unwelcome. Still Arthur believed he could make a name for himself in tennis. After all, Jackie Robinson had broken the color barrier in baseball. Arthur's teachers and coaches were very supportive and told him to seize any opportunity that came his way.

Despite his success on the court, Arthur still felt alone because he was black. "I don't belong anywhere," he once told *Sports Illustrated* magazine. "It's like I'm floating down the middle. I'm never quite sure where I am."

On the court, Arthur seemed calm, but between matches he often suffered nervous cramps. His health was always a concern, and in 1979, he suffered a major heart attack. He underwent surgery but still suffered from chest pains. In April, 1980, Arthur retired from tennis.

In 1992, Arthur attended a Tennis Challenge benefit for the Arthur Ashe Foundation for the Defeat of AIDS with his daughter, Camera.

Arthur's health continued to get worse. He had another heart operation in 1983 and a brain operation in 1988. Tests after the brain surgery showed he had AIDS, an incurable disease. He had caught the disease through a blood transfusion during his 1983 heart surgery.

A quilt honoring the memory of Arthur Ashe was displayed at the 1993 Berlin AIDS conference.

At first, Arthur told only his wife and other close family members about the disease. However, in 1992, because there were rumors about it in the newspapers, Arthur told the public. In his few remaining months, Arthur spoke to different groups about AIDS. Shortly before he died in 1993, he set up the Arthur Ashe Foundation for the Defeat of AIDS.

Special Interests

- Arthur spent $250,000 of his own money and devoted several years to researching and writing a three-volume history of America's black athletes entitled *A Hard Road to Glory*. It was later adapted for television.
- Arthur was part of a group that successfully got South Africa banned from the Davis Cup because of the government's racist policies.
- Arthur was an avid book collector. He used to order books from rare book dealers in New York, Boston, and Chicago.

Earvin "Magic" Johnson

Family: Married Earletha "Cookie" Kelly, 1991. Has two children, Andre and Earvin III.

Education: Attended Michigan State University, 1977-79.

Awards: Named NBA championship series Most Valuable Player, 1979, 1980; Schick Pivotal Player Award, 1984; named NBA league's Most Valuable Player, 1987; named NBA All Star Game's Most Valuable Player, 1992; Olympic gold medal, 1992.

Personality Profile

Career: Basketball player and head coach.

Born: August 14, 1959, in Lansing, Michigan, to Earvin, Sr. and Christine Johnson.

Growing Up

F ree time was rare for Magic's parents in Lansing, Michigan. His father, Earvin, Sr., often worked at two jobs, and his mother, Christine, worked in a school cafeteria to support their ten children. Whenever Earvin, Sr. finally had some spare time, he and Earvin, Jr., as Magic was then known, would watch basketball on television and discuss different strategies.

As soon as Magic saw a new move on television, he wanted to try it. He would practice before and after school, dribbling in between cars, pretending they were other players. Before he started to grow tall, Magic was chubby. People in the neighborhood called him June Bug because he was always hopping around practicing basketball moves. But all those hours of practicing would pay off one day.

When Magic arrived at Lansing Everett High School, he didn't know any other students. At first, he seemed moody and sulky. Once the basketball season began, Magic quickly made friends, and, as the team's high scorer, he soon became the school hero. His mood changed, and Magic became known for his easy nature and broad smile.

In 1978, Magic played for the Michigan State University Spartans. Here he rushes past a University of Kentucky forward in a drive for the basket.

As a senior at Lansing Everett High School, Magic led his team to the Class A championship finals which they won. In 1974, a local sports reporter wrote that Magic could do "magic"on the court, and the nickname stuck. But some of his teammates felt that Magic was becoming a show-off. He realized that a team effort was the answer and learned the passing game which would make him famous.

Developing Skills

While a freshman at Michigan State University, Magic led the college basketball team, the Spartans, to the 1977-78 Big Ten championships. The Spartans advanced to the 1979 National Collegiate Athletic Association (NCAA) championship final and won. Magic won the Most Valuable Player (MVP) award in the championships and signed with the Los Angeles Lakers.

Magic in a Lakers game in 1991.

Magic was a breath of fresh air to the Lakers. His confidence and good mood rubbed off on his teammates, and the next year Magic led the team to a first-place finish in their division. They then won the National Basketball Association (NBA) championship for the first time since 1972.

Magic finished his first season with a .530 shooting percentage, 563 assists, a free-throw percentage of .810, and an average of 18 points a game. His most exciting moment took place in the sixth game of the finals. When the regular center, Kareem Abdul-Jabbar, was injured, Magic stepped in. He scored 42 points, grabbed 15 rebounds, had seven assists, three steals, and a blocked shot. He was named the series Most Valuable Player.

The next year began badly for Magic. First he injured his knee and missed forty-six games. Then some of his teammates resented the $25-million, 25-year contract Magic signed with the Lakers. When Magic and the head coach disagreed about strategy, and the coach was fired, fellow Lakers began to wonder if Magic had too much say in running the team. However, the Lakers won the NBA championship, and Magic again was named the series Most Valuable Player.

The Lakers went on to win the championship in 1985, 1987, and 1988. Magic became a star. He was mobbed by loyal fans wherever he went. Soon he traveled with bodyguards and lived in a fenced-in, guarded estate.

In 1991, Magic was diagnosed as having the virus that leads to AIDS. Rumors of his illness soon appeared in the newspapers and on television. On November 7, 1991, Magic called together his teammates to tell them the bad news. "There was never any question that I would go public with this," Magic wrote in his autobiography. "Maybe I could have kept it quiet, but I doubt it. Besides, I've never lied to people, and I didn't want to start now. I've always lived straight ahead, facing up to whatever happens." After telling his teammates about his disease, Magic told his story at a press conference. The news stunned the world.

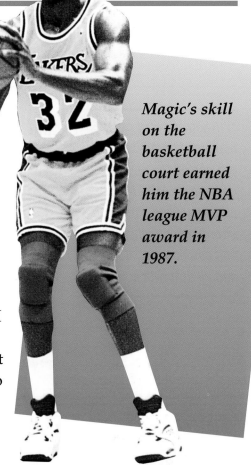

Magic's skill on the basketball court earned him the NBA league MVP award in 1987.

Accomplishments

1978 Led Michigan State University Spartans to the Big Ten championship. Set a school record with 269 assists.

1979 Joined Los Angeles Lakers, won NBA championship, and named series MVP.

1980 Led Lakers to NBA championship, and won series MVP.

1983 Published autobiography, Magic.

1984 Won Schick Pivotal Player Award.

1987 Named league MVP.

1991 Became spokesperson for AIDS awareness.

1992 Named MVP of NBA All Star Game, won gold medal with U.S. Olympic team.

1994 Named the Lakers' head coach.

Overcoming Obstacles

Magic was a superstar on the basketball court, but early in his career many of his teammates did not get on with him. Several of them were jealous of his talent. When Magic signed a $25-million, 25-year contract with the team, his teammates thought he was getting too much power over the team.

These problems were minor compared with what Magic faced when doctors told him he carried the HIV virus which leads to AIDS. But Magic has responded by becoming a spokesperson for AIDS awareness, traveling to schools and youth clubs and talking to young people. He also joined the President's National Commission on AIDS. "I want (kids) to understand that safe sex is the way to go," he told *People* magazine."Sometimes we think only gay people can get it, or that it's not going to happen to me. And I'm saying it can happen to anybody, even Magic Johnson." In 1992, Magic left the commission because he felt President Bush was not paying enough attention to their work.

"I'm actually glad (AIDS) happened to me. I think I can spread the message concerning AIDS better than almost anyone. I'm a super strong person, physically and emotionally. I'll take it and I'll deal with it."

Magic met with President George Bush in 1992 when Magic belonged to the President's National Commision on AIDS.

Magic decided to keep in shape to overcome the effects of his disease. He wanted to play in the 1992 NBA All-Star game. Some players felt that he might have lost his touch. Others felt a retired player should not be allowed to play. Magic surprised them all. He stepped onto the court, and the crowd gave him a two-minute standing ovation. He scored twenty-five points, pulled down five rebounds, and made two steals. He proved to the world that a person with the AIDS virus can still be productive.

Early in 1992, Magic's number was retired in a ceremony at the Los Angeles Forum. But his career did not end there. During the summer of 1992, he played for the U.S. Olympic team in Spain, and the team won the gold medal. Magic hoped to rejoin the Lakers for the 1993 season, but his friends and doctors convinced him not to.

In March, 1994, Magic was reunited with his former teammates when he became the Lakers' head coach.

In 1991, Magic announced at a press conference that he had HIV, the virus that causes AIDS.

Special Interests

- Magic works with the Special Olympics Program. He also founded a special "Active Reading" program in his hometown to help students with reading problems.
- Helped organize a fund-raiser which provided $200,000 for the United Negro College Fund.

Michael Jordan

Personality Profile

Career: Basketball player and baseball player.

Born: February 17, 1963, in Brooklyn, New York, to James and Deloris Jordan.

Family: Married Juanita Vanoy, 1989. Has three children, Jeffrey, Marcus, and Jasmine.

Education: Attended University of North Carolina at Chapel Hill (UNC), 1981-84.

Awards: Unanimous Selection First Team All American, 1982-83, 1983-84; Collegiate Player of the Year, 1983, 1984; Rookie of the Year, National Basetball Association, 1985; Seagram's Player of the Year, 1987; NBA Most Valuable Player, 1988, 1991, 1992, 1993; NBA scoring champion, 1987, 1988, 1989, 1990, 1991, 1992, 1993.

Growing Up

By the time he was in grade nine, Michael knew he wanted to be a basketball player. He was too short to make the varsity team, so he spent hours each day practicing his jump shot. The next year he was six inches taller, had improved his skills, and made the team. Michael became such a good player that he was invited to spend a summer at the Five-Star Basketball Camp in Pittsburgh, Pennsylvania, a school for the country's best high-school players. Scouts visiting the camp were so impressed with Michael that they offered him scholarships to college. Michael accepted a basketball scholarship from the University of North Carolina at Chapel Hill (UNC).

Michael made the starting team at UNC, a rare thing for most first-year players. His finest moment that year came on March 29, 1982. With only seconds left on the clock and his team losing by two points, Michael sunk a sixteen-foot jump shot. His team won the National Collegiate Athletic Association (NCAA) championship for the first time in twenty-five years.

"I try to be a role model for black kids, white kids, yellow kids, green kids."

Michael continued to impress basketball fans. He was named an All-American player and *Sporting News* magazine selected him the player of the year in 1983 and 1984. He also helped the U.S. team win gold medals at the 1983 Pan American games and the 1984 Summer Olympics.

Developing Skills

After the 1984 Olympics, Michael decided to become a professional basketball player. He signed on with the losing Chicago Bulls of the National Basketball Association (NBA) and became known for his wild dunk shots, dribbling skills, and shooting ability. Fans soon nicknamed his performance on the court "The Michael Jordan Air Show." Michael put the Bulls in the playoffs, and he finished his first season as the league's 1985 Rookie of the Year.

Michael during a 1992 NBA finals game against the Portland Trailblazers.

The next season Michael broke his foot and missed most of the games. But he rebounded in 1989 by becoming the second NBA player ever to score more than 3,000 points in a season. He also set a record by scoring eighteen straight points in a game against the New York Knicks.

By 1988, Michael had reached superstar status. He was the league's Most Valuable Player, the Defensive Player of the Year, and was the Most Valuable Player at the annual All-Star Game.

Michael and the Chicago Bulls continued to do well, but they were not able to win a championship. In 1990, they were defeated by the Detroit Pistons in the first round of the playoffs. Michael played well, but the rest of the team did not. Michael accused his teammates of not trying hard enough, while they said he wanted all the glory and would not pass to them when they had a chance to score.

The next year Michael decided to hold back his own play and started setting up his teammates. The plan worked. The Bulls finished first in their division and Michael was named the league's Most Valuable Player.

In the playoffs, the Bulls steamrolled past their opponents, winning fifteen of seventeen games including the championship. Michael was named the series Most Valuable Player. "I don't know if I'll ever have this same feeling again," Michael later told reporters. "It's been a seven-year struggle for me and the city of Chicago. And we did it as a team; all season long we did it as a team."

Michael speaking at a luncheon in Charlotte, South Carolina.

Accomplishments

1982 Made UNC's starting lineup; led team to first NCAA championship in twenty-five years.

1983 Led U.S. team to gold medal at Pan American games; named *Sporting News* Player of the Year.

1984 Led U.S. team to gold medal at Summer Olympics; joined Chicago Bulls; named NBA's Rookie of the Year.

1985 Signed with Nike to promote a special line of basketball shoes called "Air Jordan."

1987 Became second NBA player in history to score more than 3,000 points in a season; set a record eighteen straight points in a game.

1988 Named NBA Most Valuable Player (MVP), Defensive Player of the Year, and Most Valuable Player at the annual All-Star Game.

1990 Bulls win NBA championship, Michael named league MVP and playoff MVP.

Overcoming Obstacles

Michael's career was the stuff of dreams. He became the most popular basketball player in the world. He made a lot of money by promoting sports equipment. He became the spokesman for Nike shoes, tote bags, gym shorts, T-shirts, and sweatshirts. This led to other promotions for Wheaties, Coca-Cola, Gatorade, McDonald's, and the Illinois State Lottery. He was famous, popular, and a superstar on the basketball court, but in 1993, at age thirty, he walked away from the game.

His decision remains a bit of a mystery. "There's nothing left for me to prove," Michael said at the time. "I can't step out on the court and know it's for no reason. It's not worth it for me. It's not worth it for my teammates."

Some people feel the death of his father influenced Michael's decision to retire. Michael's father was his greatest supporter, and his loss was a terrible blow to Michael.

"If I lost my talent tomorrow, I'd say I had a great time and move on. I live for today but plan for the future."

Michael decided to take up a new challenge in 1994 when he tried out for the Chicago White Sox baseball team. He did not make the team, but he started playing baseball in the minor leagues with the Birmingham Barons. Although Michael was a good baseball player, he did not have as much success as he had with basketball. To make things worse, a long baseball strike wiped out the 1994 season, and Michael could not play.

During the strike, Michael began to think about basketball again. On March 19, 1995, eighteen months after he had left, he returned to basketball when he signed on again with the Chicago Bulls.

One of Michael's business ventures is Michael Jordan's The Restaurant.

Special Interests

- Michael established the Michael Jordan Foundation which donates money to charities which help children.
- Michael spends his free time visiting sick children, lecturing on drug abuse, holding summer camps for underprivileged children, and gives away tickets to children he meets in tough neighborhoods around the Chicago stadium.
- Michael raises money for the United Negro College Fund by organizing the Michael Jordan Celebrity Golf Classic.
- Michael kept a promise he had made to his mother years earlier by going back to college during several off-seasons. He finally received his degree from the University of North Carolina.

Jackie Joyner-Kersee

Personality Profile

Career: Heptathlete star and track-and-field athlete.

Born: March 3, 1962, in East St. Louis, Illinois, to Alfred and Mary Joyner.

Family: Married Bob Kersee, 1986.

Education: University of California, Los Angeles (UCLA).

Awards: James E. Sullivan Award for Most Outstanding Amateur Athlete, 1986; Broderick Cup for Collegiate Woman Athlete of the Year, 1986; Olympic silver medal, 1984; gold medal, Goodwill Games, 1986; gold medals in heptathlon and long jump, World Track and Field Championships, 1987; two Olympic gold medals, 1988.

Growing Up

Jackie after winning the gold medal at the 1988 Summer Olympics in Seoul, South Korea.

Jackie grew up in a rough part of East St. Louis, Illinois, where there was a lot of crime and drugs on the street. Her parents had little money and few opportunities for a better life. Jackie was determined to be a winner and not to become like many of her neighbors. When she was nine, she joined the track-and-field team at the community center on her street.

When she was fourteen, she watched the Summer Olympics on television and became a fan of American sprinter Evelyn Ashford. Jackie decided she too would go to the Olympics one day. Through her teen years, Jackie practiced during her spare time. Her mother did not want her to start dating until she was eighteen, so sports became very important to Jackie as she grew older.

Jackie's long hours of practice soon paid off. In 1976, she competed in the five track-and-field events of the pentathlon in the Junior Olympics and won— something she would do three more times. In her junior year, she set an Illinois state high school long jump record of 20 feet, 7 1/2 inches. In her spare time, she also played basketball and volleyball. Jackie graduated in 1980 in the top ten percent of her class.

Jackie was offered a scholarship from the University of California, Los Angeles (UCLA). She joined the track-and-field team and earned a spot on the U.S. Olympic team in the long jump. Jackie hoped to compete in the 1980 Olympic games but never made it because the U.S. team boycotted the event. The Soviet Union had just invaded Afghanistan, and to show that they did not approve, the United States decided not to send athletes to the games in Moscow.

"We didn't think we were poor. We didn't have a lot, but we knew our mother and father were doing their very best."

Developing Skills

While Jackie was training for the upcoming 1984 Olympics, Bob Kersee became her coach. Bob realized that Jackie had great potential as an athlete and convinced her to start competing in the heptathlon. The heptathlon consists of the 200-and 800-meter dashes, the 100-meter hurdles, the high jump, long jump, shot put, and javelin thrown. Later, in 1986, Bob and Jackie were married.

Jackie's athletic skills continued to improve, and she qualified for the 1983 world track-and-field championships in Helsinki, Finland. But before she could compete, she pulled a hamstring muscle in her leg and had to withdraw from the competition.

Jackie in the heptathlon long jump at a meet in 1988 in Indianapolis.

The same leg problem followed Jackie the next year at the Olympic games in Los Angeles. Because of her injury she fell thirty points behind the heptathlon leader during the first day. It would take a miracle to come back and win the gold medal. Jackie narrowed the gap the next day by winning the javelin throw. The race for the gold eventually came down to the final event, the 800-meter run. Jackie finished just .06 seconds behind the time she needed to win the gold medal. She had to settle for the silver.

Jackie knew that she was good enough to win the gold medal. She trained even harder for the 1988 Olympics in Seoul, South Korea. In 1986, she broke the world record at the Goodwill Games in Moscow. She was the first athlete in history to break the 7,000-point mark in the heptathlon. Less than a month later, she broke her record at the U.S. Olympic Festival. In 1987, she won gold medals in the heptathlon and long jump at the world track-and-field championships in Rome, Italy.

All of this training set the stage for the 1988 Olympic games. Jackie did not disappoint her fans. She won gold medals in the heptathlon and long jump. She also broke her own heptathlon record. Jackie, along with her sister-in-law, Florence Griffith Joyner, shared the spotlight at the games by each winning three gold medals.

Jackie with a bouquet of flowers after winning the gold medal in the women's heptathlon at the 1988 Summer Olympics in Seoul, South Korea.

Accomplishments

1976-79 Won National Junior Pentathlon Championship four years in a row.

1980 Earned spot on U.S. Olympic team.

1983 Qualified for world track-and-field championships but unable to compete due to injury.

1984 Won silver medal at Olympic games in Los Angeles, California.

1986 Won gold medal at Goodwill Games in Moscow, set world record in heptathlon.

1987 Won gold medals in heptathlon and long jump at the world track-and-field championships in Rome, Italy.

1988 Won gold medal in the heptathlon and long jump at the Olympic games in Seoul, South Korea, and set new heptathlon record. East St. Louis, Illinois, named a day in her honor.

Overcoming Obstacles

By the time Jackie was twelve, she could jump over seventeen feet.

Considering her early years, it is hard to believe that today Jackie is a world-class athlete. She was born to teenage parents who lived in a shack. The family had to sleep in the kitchen near the stove to stay warm, and there was little food in the house.

Jackie was determined to escape this poverty. At age nine, she entered her first track meet but came in last. Jackie knew she could do better and began practicing. After only a week she had improved. Before long, she was winning, especially in the long jump.

Although her family had little money, they wanted to support Jackie in every way. They built a long jump pit at the end of their porch. Jackie and her sisters collected old potato chip bags, filled them with sand from a nearby playground, and emptied them into the pit.

Jackie practiced constantly and soon could see the results of her dedication. The more she trained the better she got. She became an inspiration to her brother, Alfred, Jr., who grew up to win an Olympic gold medal in the triple jump.

But Jackie still found time for her school work and was an excellent student. Although her parents fully supported her athletic training, they insisted she do well at school. She was not allowed out until her homework was finished, and if her marks were bad, her parents grounded her.

Jackie in 1991 in the high jump at the world track-and-field championships in Tokyo, Japan.

Another problem Jackie faces is that she suffers from asthma, a lung condition which makes it difficult to breathe especially when she is exercising in cold weather. Because of the problem of athletes not taking certain drugs, Jackie has to be very careful about what medicine she takes.

Jackie has not forgotten her roots. She raised $40,000 in East St. Louis to reopen the Mary Brown Community Center where she began her track-and-field career. She talks to youths and civic groups in her hometown and tours across the country speaking to young people, telling them that with hard work their dream can become real.

Despite her busy schedule, Jackie continues her training. She hopes to be part of the U.S. team at the 1996 Summer Olympics in Atlanta, Georgia.

Special Interests

- In 1989, Jackie spent 216 days traveling around the country.
- She started the Jackie Joyner-Kersee Community Foundation for disadvantaged inner-city children.

Carl Lewis

Personality Profile

Career: Track-and-field athlete.

Born: July 1, 1961, Birmingham, Alabama, to Bill and Evelyn Lewis.

Education: University of Houston.

Awards: Four Olympic gold medals, 1984; Jesse Owens Award, 1985; two Olympic gold medals, 1988; two Olympic gold medals, 1992.

Growing Up

It seemed only natural that Carl would become an athlete. His father, Bill, had run track and had been a star football player at college, while his mother, Evelyn, had been a hurdler in the 1951 Pan American Games. When Carl was born, the Lewises were living in Birmingham, Alabama, but they soon moved to a suburb of Philadelphia and started a track-and-field club.

When Carl was eight, he began going to the club, but he was skinny and small and not a very good athlete. For a while, his parents tried to persuade him to take music lessons instead. But Carl was determined to be a track-and-field athlete. He went home and measured off 29 feet, 2 1/2 inches of his back yard and marked the length with tape. This was a distance that not even the best long jumpers could make. Then he began to practice. At first he lost more meets than he won.

Carl setting a record in 1978 at the national junior championships in the long jump with a leap of 23 feet, 6 inches.

Four years later, in 1973, Carl's practicing began to pay off when he won the long jump at the Jesse Owens Youth Program in Philadelphia. In 1978, Carl ran the 100-meter dash in 9.3 seconds and set a national high school record in long jump. In his senior year, Carl was the top-ranked high school track athlete in the country.

Developing Skills

Carl won an athletic scholarship from the University of Houston in Texas. Here he met coach Tom Tellez who pointed out several weak points in his long-jump style. Tom told Carl that his last four strides to the pit were too long. He explained that, besides slowing him down, these strides caused Carl's knee to swell. Carl began to practice a new style. Within a year, he qualified for the 1980 U.S. Olympic team. But Carl never got a chance to compete because the U.S. boycotted the Moscow Olympics in response to the Soviet Union's invasion of Afghanistan.

Carl continued to compete in local meets. In 1981, he won the 100-meter and long jump events at the National Collegiate Athletic Association championships. It was the first time anyone had ever won two track-and-field events in this championship. Carl repeated his success at the U.S. outdoor track-and-field championships in Sacramento, California, and again at the national outdoor championships in Knoxville, Tennessee.

In 1982, Carl left university and began to train at the Santa Monica Track Club in California. He continued to improve.

Carl in 1981 after winning the long jump at the National Collegiate Athletic Association indoor championships.

In 1983, Carl showed the world he was ready for the 1984 Olympics by winning three gold medals at the track-and-field world championships in Helsinki, Finland. A few months later, Carl broke the world indoor long-jump record with a distance of 28 feet, 10 1/2 inches.

In 1984, Carl finally got his chance to compete in the Olympic games in Los Angeles, California. He won four gold medals in the 100-meter sprint, the 200-meter dash, the long jump, and the 400-meter relay. Four years later, in the Olympic games in Seoul, Korea, he won two more gold medals. In 1992, he won two Olympic gold and one silver medal at the games in Barcelona, Spain.

Carl at the 1984 Summer Olympics in Los Angeles.

Accomplishments

1973 Won the long jump at a Jesse Owens Youth Program meet.

1978 Set a national high school long-jump record at the national junior championships.

1981 Won the 100-meter and long jump at the National Collegiate Athletic Association indoor championships.

1983 Won the 100-meter and set a world record in the long jump at the Athletics Congress outdoor championship. Won three gold medals at the world track-and-field championships in Helsinki, Finland.

1984 Won four gold medals at the Olympic games in Los Angeles, California.

1988 Won two gold and a silver medal at the Olympic games at Seoul, South Korea.

1992 Won the long jump and 400-meter relay at the Olympic games in Barcelona, Spain.

Overcoming Obstacles

Carl in the long jump competition at the 1992 Summer Olympics in Barcelona, Spain.

Many sports fans thought Carl was ready for retirement in 1988 after he had won six Olympic gold medals and had set world records for the long jump. He was twenty-seven years old and most people believed he had passed his peak years of performance. But Carl decided he wanted to compete once more in the 1992 Olympics in Barcelona, Spain. It would be a difficult task.

Although Carl practiced a lot, he failed to make the U.S. team in the 100-and 200-meter dash. He just managed to make the long-jump team and was also named an alternate for the relay team. Little was expected of him, but Carl surprised his competitors and the world. He won his seventh Olympic gold medal in the long jump, and when a teammate suffered an injury, Carl helped the 400-meter relay team win a gold medal. He was thirty-one years old.

Besides the constant pressure of competition, Carl had other obstacles to overcome during his career. He was very ambitious and boasted to the press before events that he would win. Many sports fans did not like Carl's attitude, and he got bad reports in the press. Even when he won four gold medals in 1984, he was criticized for not setting any records.

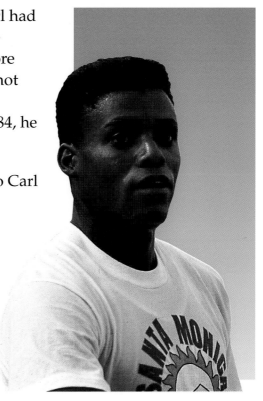

After Ben Johnson lost his Olympic gold medal to Carl because Ben had taken steroids, Carl was also accused of taking illegal drugs. He denied the charge and was always ready to take drug tests after his races. Never was any proof of his taking drugs found.

Carl's greatest challenge may be getting used to being away from the track. Shortly after the 1992 Olympics, Carl, "best track-and-field athlete ever," retired.

"I have made it through the roadblocks by looking forward, and that is why I will always be comfortable with who I am."

Special Interests

- Carl's success on the track has made him a millionaire. Along with the prize money he has received, Carl has also made several commercials and numerous personal appearances.
- Carl has made many statements against steroid drug use. He denies ever having used steroids and encourages young athletes to win without drugs.
- Carl owns a line of sportswear called "Sports Style."

Willie Mays

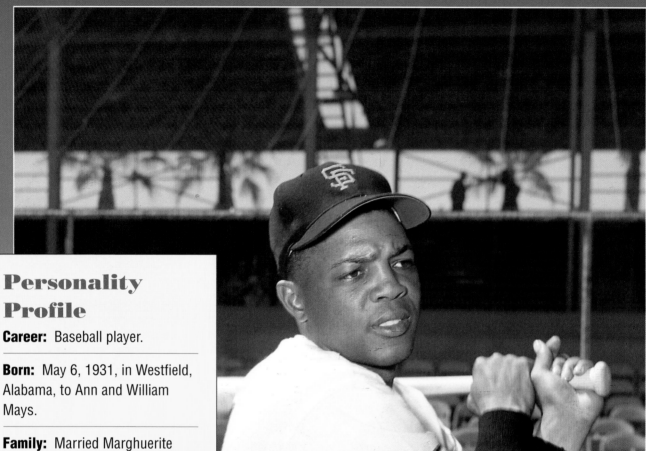

Personality Profile

Career: Baseball player.

Born: May 6, 1931, in Westfield, Alabama, to Ann and William Mays.

Family: Married Marghuerite Wendell, 1958, (divorced, 1963); married Mae Louise Allen, 1971. Has a son, Michael.

Education: Diploma from Fairfield Industrial High School.

Awards: Rookie of the Year, 1951; National League Most Valuable Player, 1954; League Stolen Base Champion, 1956–59; National League Most Valuable Player, 1965; inducted into Baseball Hall of Fame, 1979.

Growing Up

It seems Willie was born to play baseball. His father, William Howard Mays, Sr., a steel worker, played center field for the local semi-professional team. His mother, Ann, had been a high school track star. As soon as Willie learned to walk, his father began teaching him how to throw, catch, and hit a baseball.

After his parents divorced when he was three, Willie lived with his father and kept playing baseball. As Willie grew older, he realized baseball could be a good career and would give him a future other than working in the steelmills. Willie, Sr. encouraged his son to learn more about the sport. Willie spent most of his time on the baseball field, playing ball or sitting in the dugout with his father, listening to baseball strategy and getting tips on how to improve his game. By the time he was thirteen, Willie was playing on a semi-professional team called the Gray Sox.

Before too long, Willie was playing center field on his father's team. Willie was such a good player that his friends told him to try out for the Birmingham Black Barons, a team in the Negro Leagues, the major league for black players. This was 1947, and at that time blacks and whites did not play baseball together. The Negro Leagues played in the southern states and in some northern cities.

Although he was only fifteen, Willie made the team. He played with men who were ten years older, and was paid $250 a month, which was much more than other high school students made.

"My idea was to do everything better than anybody else ever had. I concentrated on every aspect of the game."

Developing Skills

In the late 1940s, the major leagues had just begun letting black players on their teams and were sending scouts to the Negro Leagues to find good players. A scout for the New York Giants saw Willie and was impressed with his skills. The Giants offered Willie a contract to play for their minor league team. He was only nineteen, but his playing immediately attracted the fans' attention. Not only did he have a high batting average, but he was also making amazing plays in the outfield.

Willie at bat for the Giants.

The next year, the New York Giants began their season badly, so manager Leo Durocher decided to call Willie to the team. On May 25, 1951, Willie, a shy and nervous rookie, began his long career with the Giants as starting center fielder and number three hitter. At first, Willie and the team played poorly and were thirteen-and-a-half games from first place. Then towards the end of the season, they won sixteen games in a row and forced a sudden-death playoff with the first-place Brooklyn Dodgers. The Giants won the playoff but lost the World Series to the New York Yankees in seven games. Willie's 20 home runs and .274 batting average were good enough to win him the National League's Rookie of the Year award.

Many fans felt Willie had superstar potential. But in 1952, Willie was drafted into the U.S. Army. For two years, he served as a baseball instructor for their baseball teams. When he came back to the major leagues, many people wondered if the time off had hurt his skills.

Those worries were soon put to rest. Willie led the Giants to a world championship in 1954 with a .345 batting average and 41 home runs, and he won the Most Valuable Player award. He made such a great fielding play in that year's World Series that ever since then it is simply called "the catch." Willie had become the superstar that many had predicted. With his incredible gift of speed and power, he could hit hard, steal bases, and field balls equally well.

After the 1957 season, the Giants moved to San Francisco, California. Willie played baseball until 1973, when he finally retired from the game after twenty-two seasons, one of the greatest all-round players in baseball history.

Willie's great fielding play in the 1954 World Series became known as "the catch."

Accomplishments

Year	Event	Year	Event
1950	Signed with New York Giants Class A team	**1969**	Hit 600th home run.
1951	Joined New York Giants. Named National League's Rookie of the Year. Giants won pennant.	**1973**	Retired with 660 home runs, second only to Babe Ruth.
1954	Giants won World Series. Won Most Valuable Player Award.	**1979**	Voted into Baseball Hall of Fame.
1965	Hit 500th home run. Won Most Valuable Player Award.	**1988**	Wrote *Say Hey: The Autobiography of Willie Mays*.

Overcoming Obstacles

Although Jackie Robinson had broken the color barrier in major league baseball, many black players still suffered from racism when Willie began his career. Willie was no exception. As a member of the Black Barons, Willie and the rest of the team would often have to ride all night in their secondhand bus, traveling to the next day's game. When they reached the city where they were to play, they had to stay in second-class, blacks-only hotels. But Willie did not mind. He just wanted to play baseball, and the conditions did not matter to him.

Willie's career was not without its setbacks. When he first started playing with the Giants, it looked as if he might not have enough talent to be a professional. He had only one hit in twenty-five times at bat. Many thought that the Giants' manager, Leo Durocher, had made a mistake in bringing Willie onto the team. But Durocher was like a father to Willie and never doubted his talent. If it had not been for Durocher's faith, Willie may never have stayed in the major leagues.

Many doubted the Giants' manager's decision to bring Willie onto the team, but Willie eventually proved his talent.

"If I get thrown out of the game, I'll only hurt the club," Willie explained why he never argued with an umpire.

One of the constant problems Willie faced was poor health. Baseball life was hectic, with constant travel, jet-lag, airplane food, and pressure from the press. Willie tried so hard to chase after balls, steal bases, and hit home runs that he was often exhausted and suffered from fainting spells. Once he even collapsed while standing at the plate.

Perhaps the biggest challenge Willie faced was when the Giants left New York for San Francisco. The fans in New York had cheered Willie as a hero, but in San Francisco he was just another player. He had to prove his worth all over again. This was no easy task. Willie played in center field, and, at Candlestick Park in San Francisco, the high winds blew the ball in all directions. Eventually Willie was able to figure out the new park. Soon he began to shine at bat and in the field and was again greeted as a hero by the fans.

Willie's nickname was the "Say Hey Kid" because he greeted fans and friends with "Say Hey!"

Special Interests

- In his retirement, Willie became a keen golfer.
- Willie set up a foundation to help put students of all races through school and college.
- Despite his busy schedule, Willie often had time to play stickball with kids on the streets of Harlem.
- Willie loves to travel to baseball-card shows and sign cards for his fans.

Zina Garrison

She often followed Rodney to the playground and soon began hanging around the tennis courts, watching coach John Wilkerson give private lessons.

Tragedy hit Zina's family in 1964 when she was an eleventh-month-old baby. Her father died suddenly of a stroke, and, a few months later, her older brother died after he was hit in the eye with a baseball. Zina became very close to her mother and her favorite brother, Rodney. Although she was a quiet child, she loved to run, dance, and play softball. She often followed Rodney to the playground and soon began hanging around the tennis courts, watching coach John Wilkerson give private lessons.

One day, John handed Zina a wooden tennis racket, showed her the basics of the game, and told her to try playing. Tennis was a perfect focus for Zina's interest in running, dancing, and softball.

John soon recognized Zina's talent and began entering her in local tournaments. She had to work extra hard to win. She did not have the advantage of some of her white opponents who had been trained by the best professionals and belonged to expensive clubs.

In 1981, when Zina was seventeen, she won the junior singles at Wimbledon and the U.S. Open tennis tournaments. John continued as her coach, and they began a hectic schedule of playing in tournaments all over the United States, Europe, and the Far East. Zina had little time to spend at home, and she worried about her mother who suffered from diabetes.

> ## Personality Profile
>
> **Career:** Tennis player.
>
> **Born:** 1963 in Houston, Texas, to Ulysses and Mary Garrison.
>
> **Awards:** Wimbledon Junior and the Junior U.S. Open, 1981; Most Impressive Newcomer, Women's International Tennis Association, 1982; won a bronze and a gold Olympic medal, 1988; French Open, 1990.

Zina was heartbroken when her mother died in 1983. She tried to forget her sorrow by putting all her energy into her tennis game. That year, she reached the semi-finals at Wimbledon, the quarter-finals at the Australian Open and the U.S. Open, and earned $274,000.

However, Zina had never dealt with her mother's death, and she started to collapse. She began to suffer from an eating disorder and went on eating binges. She had little energy, and her game was affected. In 1986, she began crying on the courts while playing a match at Wimbledon. She lost her lead and then the game.

Zina decided to pull herself together. She went to a doctor who helped her conquer her eating disorder. She began giving tennis clinics in the inner cities to disadvantaged children. Her determination paid off. She went to the 1988 Olympic games in Seoul, South Korea, and won a bronze in the singles and a gold in the doubles competitions. She had her best year in 1990, when she won the French Open and advanced to the finals at Wimbledon. She became the fourth-ranking female tennis player in the world.

Today, Zina is a multi-millionaire. She gives sports clinics, makes public appearances, and endorses sports products. As well, she devotes a lot of her time trying to introduce black children to tennis. She also works with disadvantaged young people of all races, telling them that they don't have to be athletes to succeed. They should just work hard at what they are.

Accomplishments

1981 Won both the Wimbledon Junior and U.S. Open Junior titles. Named Female Athlete of the Year by the U.S. Olympic Committee.

1984 Won the European Indoor title at Zurich, Switzerland.

1988 Won a bronze medal in women's singles and a gold medal with Pam Shriver in women's doubles at the Summer Olympic games.

1990 Won the French Open, finalist at Wimbledon.

Althea Gibson

Althea, who lived in a crowded apartment in Harlem, often got into trouble with her parents and her teachers for skipping school to go to the movies.

F ew African-American children ever played tennis when Althea was growing up in the 1930s, but one day she would be the first black, international tennis player in the world.

Althea, who lived in a crowded apartment in Harlem, often got into trouble with her parents and her teachers for skipping school to go to the movies. After junior high, she quit school and worked at a series of odd jobs such as a mail clerk and a counter girl in a restaurant. She was fired from most of her jobs because she kept skipping work and going to the movies.

Another thing Althea loved was playing basketball, stickball, and paddleball with the Police Athletic Association League which sponsored games in her neighborhood. She played fast and thrived on the competition. Buddy Walker, a musician who worked in the city recreational department in the summer, noticed Althea's talent, gave her a second-hand tennis racket, and told her to start hitting balls. Althea finally found something that really fascinated her.

Soon she was playing so well that Buddy arranged for fourteen-year-old Althea to play a few tennis games with the pro at the New York Cosmopolitan Club. Club members were so impressed with her skill that they gave her a junior membership and paid for her lessons. In a year, in 1942, Althea won her first tournament, the girls' singles in the New York State Open Championship. In 1944 and 1945, she won the girls' singles in the American Tennis Association (ATA) national tournament.

Personality Profile

Career: Tennis player.

Born: August 25, 1927, in Silver, South Carolina, to Daniel and Annie Gibson.

Education: Williston Industrial High School, 1946-49; Florida Agricultural and Mechanical College, 1949-53.

Awards: Women's champion, American Tennis Association, 1947–1956; singles and doubles champion, Wimbledon, 1957, 1958.

In 1946, at the age of eighteen, Althea was eligible to enter the women's singles at the ATA. She lost but was noticed by Hubert Eaton, an African-American surgeon who was a leader in the ATA. He offered to feed, clothe, and send Althea to school at his own expense. She agreed and went to live with the Eatons in Wilmington, North Carolina. She returned to school and in her spare time practiced on the Eaton's private tennis court, the only one for blacks in the city. During the summer, she traveled to tournaments. The next year, and for the next nine years, Althea won the ATA women's championship.

In 1949, Althea graduated tenth in her class and entered Florida Agricultural College on a tennis scholarship. For the next four years, she focused on her studies and continued to play tennis. She became the first black person to play at Forest Hills, a famous tournament in Long Island, New York. After Althea graduated from college, she put tennis on hold and taught physical education at Lincoln University in Missouri. Two years later, she returned to the game, playing around the world and winning sixteen out of eighteen tournaments.

In 1957, Althea became the first black woman to compete and win in singles and in doubles at the world-famous tennis tournament at Wimbledon in England. She also won the women's singles at Forest Hills. The next year, she returned to Wimbledon and won again.

Althea retired from tennis in 1959. She became a singer, actress, and a professional golfer, playing in several tournaments. Although she never became rich playing tennis, she opened the door for many African Americans to follow in her footsteps.

Accomplishments

1942 Won the girls' singles in the New York State Open Championship.

1947 Won the American Tennis Association women's championship. She would win the tournament for the next nine years.

1950 Became the first black to play at Forest Hills.

1954 Graduated from Florida A & M with a degree in physical education.

1957 Became the first black woman to win the singles and doubles championships at Wimbledon.

1959 Retired from tennis. She became a singer, actress, and golfer.

Shaquille O'Neal

During Shaquille's last year at high school, his father told him he was not trying hard enough.

I magine being 6 feet 6 inches tall and wearing size seventeen shoes when you are only thirteen years old. That's how big Shaquille was, and he kept growing so fast in his teenage years that he sometimes outgrew his clothes in a few weeks.

Shaquille was born and raised in a rough area of Newark, New Jersey. In 1984, when he was twelve, he moved with his parents to a military base in West Germany where his father was sent by the U.S. Army.

In 1987, Shaquille's family moved to San Antonio, Texas, and he enrolled at Cole High School. By this time, he was 6 feet 10 inches tall and weighed 250 pounds. His size naturally brought him to the basketball court, and he led the school team to a 32-1 win/loss record. But he was not yet considered an outstanding prospect. During Shaquille's last year at high school, his father told him he was not trying hard enough. The next game, Shaquille scored 52 points, and Cole High went on to win the Texas state title.

Several colleges were interested in Shaquille and offered him scholarships. He chose to attend Louisiana State University (LSU) because he had met the coach, Dale Brown, a few years earlier at a basketball camp.

When Shaquille joined LSU in 1989, he found himself surrounded by talented players such as Stanley Roberts and Chris Jackson. It was tough for Shaquille, who had become used to being the team star.

Just a year later, Shaquille was making headlines for his exceptional play in the National Sports Festival. Playing in a tournament against much older players, Shaquille was named the most valuable player. He averaged 24.5 points and 13.8 rebounds per game.

When he returned to LSU, things were different for Shaquille. Teammates Stanley Roberts and Chris Jackson had moved on, and Shaquille was named co-captain. His vertical jump of 42 inches made him a college superstar. He led the National Collegiate Athletic Association (NCAA) in 1990-91 with 15.2 rebounds per game, was sixth in scoring (25.8 points), and fourth in blocked shots (4.8). His size and his skill in controlling the ball were the keys to his success.

Coach Brown recognized Shaquille's talent and asked Kareem Abdul-Jabbar and Bill Walton, two former National Basketball Association stars, to teach Shaquille a few basketball tricks. Kareem taught him his famous sky hook, and Bill showed him shot-blocking.

Personality Profile

Career: Basketball player.

Born: March 6, 1972, in Newark, New Jersey to Lucille O'Neal and Philip Harrison.

Education: Attended Cole High School, 1987-89; Louisiana State University, 1989-92.

Awards: Most Valuable Player, National Sports Festival, 1990; Rookie of the Year, National Basketball Association, 1993.

Feeling he had nothing more to prove at LSU, Shaquille decided to enter the NBA draft during his senior year. The Orlando Magic made him the first overall draft pick, and he signed for a reported $40 million over seven years. He also worked out a deal with a trading card company for $1 million. Shaquille did not disappoint his new team. He has gone on to become not only a star with the Magic, but also in the entire league. He finished his first season as the NBA Rookie of the Year.

In 1994, Shaquille branched out into the entertainment business. He appeared as a basketball player in *Blue Chips*, a film about a basketball coach and his team.

Accomplishments

1989 Enrolled at Louisiana State University and averaged 13.9 points per game. Established a Southeastern Conference record of 115 blocked shots.

1990 Named Most Valuable Player in the National Sports Festival. He averaged 24.5 points per game. Named co-captain of the LSU team.

1991 Led the NCAA in rebounds, was sixth in scoring, fourth in blocked shots, and fourteenth in shooting.

1992 Chosen by the Orlando Magic in the NBA draft.

1993 Named Rookie of the Year in the NBA.

1994 Appeared in his first feature film, *Blue Chips*.

Jesse Owens

In junior high, Jesse ran the 100-yard dash in just ten seconds.

Jesse is remembered today as one of the world's greatest athletes. He was born in 1913, the seventh of eleven children. His grandparents had been slaves, and his parents were sharecroppers. When he was six, Jesse began helping his family pick cotton, but he was frail and thin and often too sick to work in the fields.

When Jesse was seven, his family moved to Cleveland, Ohio, hoping for a better life. After school, Jesse worked at odd jobs to help his parents pay the bills. He loved to run and in his spare time raced with his friends in the school yard.

In high school, Jesse began to develop as a sprinter, setting national records in the 100-yard and 200-yard dashes. The track coach at Ohio State finally convinced Jesse to attend university with the promise that his father would be given steady work. But Jesse was not given a scholarship and had to work at three jobs as well as studying and being a member of the track team.

On May 25, 1935, Jesse made track-and-field history. The team had traveled to Ann Arbor, Michigan, but Jesse had a back injury and was not even sure he could compete. At the last minute, he decided to try. That day Jesse set world records in the long jump, the 220-yard dash, and the 220-yard low hurdles.

The next year Jesse was a member of the U.S. Olympic team that competed in Berlin, Germany. Nazi leader Adolf Hitler bragged that his German athletes, especially German star Lutz Long, would win the track events easily. On his first long jump, Lutz set an Olympic records. Jesse was nervous and missed his first two attempts.

Personality Profile

Career: Olympic athlete and businessman.

Born: September 12, 1913, in Oakville, Alabama, to Emma and Henry Owens.

Died: March 31, 1980, in Phoenix, Arizona.

Education: Ohio State University, B.A., 1937.

Family: Married Ruth Solomon, 1931. Had three children, Gloria, Beverly, and Marlene.

Awards: Won four Olympic gold medals, 1936; Presidential Medal of Freedom, 1976; Living Legend Award, 1979; Congressional Gold Medal, 1990.

Finally, on his last attempt, Jesse beat Lutz's jump and set a new world record that lasted for twenty-five years. Lutz hugged Jesse for his outstanding jump, and the German crowd chanted Jesse's name. Adolf Hitler left the stadium in shame. Jesse went on to win three more gold medals. He won the 100-meter sprint, the 200-meter sprint, and the 400-meter relay.

When he returned home, he was welcomed with a parade in New York City. But Jesse could not find a job to pay for the rest of his college education. He had to run races against cars, horses, and motorcycles to earn money. Since he was paid for racing, he was considered a professional and unable to compete in any more Olympics.

Jesse graduated from Ohio State in 1937 and became a partner in a Cleveland dry cleaning operation. Business was good at first, but by 1940 the company had gone bankrupt, and Jesse was deep in debt.

In the mid-1950s, Jesse operated his own public relations firm called Jesse Owens & Associates. He wrote his autobiography, titled *Blackthink*, in 1970, and two years later published *I Have Changed*. Jesse developed lung cancer and, after a long stay in hospital, died on March 31, 1980.

It was only in 1976, forty years after winning the Olympics, that Jesse was finally awarded the honor he deserved. He was given the Presidential Medal of Freedom.

Accomplishments

1935 Set world records in the long jump, 220-yard dash, 220-yard low hurdles, and tied the world record in the 100-yard dash.

1936 Set new world record in long jump, won four Olympic gold medals.

1942 Became personnel director at the Ford Motor Corporation in Detroit, Michigan.

1950 Became a board member of the South Side Boys Club in Chicago. He also toured with the Harlem Globetrotters.

1956 Organized the Junior Olympic Games in Chicago.

Jackie Robinson

T here are some people who are simply natural athletes. Jackie was one of them. Jackie was born in Georgia in 1919 but moved with his mother to California after his father abandoned the family. Life there was not much easier for African Americans than in the South, and, even as a child, Jackie suffered from cruel treatment by racist whites.

Jackie was an amazing athlete. At high school he was outstanding at basketball, football, and track. He was so good that students would bring him sandwiches and dimes so they could play on his team. At college Jackie continued to excel as an all-round athlete. One season he led the United States in overall yardage gained in football, for two years he led the Pacific Coast League in basketball scoring, and he was an excellent tennis player.

After college Jackie played a season of professional football. Then he joined the army where he served for almost three years. There he met a pitcher in the Negro Leagues of baseball who told him to try out for a team. In those days black baseball players were not allowed to play in the major or minor leagues. At first, Jackie was not interested, but he thought that playing baseball might help him get a job working with underprivileged boys. So he agreed to give it a try.

Soon Jackie's skills were spotted by the Brooklyn Dodgers. The Dodgers' general manager, Branch Rickey, wanted to bring the first African American into major league baseball. He knew that person would have to be talented and brave. He told Jackie that, as the first black player in the major leagues, he would face bigoted fans, insults, and hostility. When Jackie asked him if he were looking for a person who would not be afraid to fight back, Branch Rickey replied that he was looking for someone who had the strength not to fight back. He knew that took a lot more courage.

Jackie signed with the Dodgers' minor league farm team in 1946. Many fans were curious to see the first black player in the league, and attendance on the road tripled. But the team had to cancel an exhibition trip through the southern United States because southern laws made it illegal for blacks and whites to play on the same field. Jackie led the league that season with a .349 batting average and a field average of .985. When his team won the pennant, fans carried Jackie on their shoulders.

Personality Profile

Career: Baseball player.

Born: January 31, 1919, in Cairo, Georgia, to Gerry and Mallie Robinson.

Died: October 24, 1972, in Stamford, Connecticut.

Education: Muir Technicial High School; Pasadena Junior College; University of California, Los Angeles.

Awards: Rookie of the Year, 1948; National League's Most Valuable Player, 1949; elected to Baseball Hall of Fame, 1962.

Jackie made it to the Dodgers' major league team the next year. Some players did not want him on the team and asked to be traded. The St. Louis Cardinals and the Philadelphia Phillies threatened not to play their games against the Dodgers. National League president Ford Frick said that if players went on strike, they would be kicked out of the league.

Jackie's first season was a success. He was named the National League's Rookie of the Year and helped the Dodgers win the league pennant. The next year, things began getting easier for Jackie, and he went on to become one of the best hitters and base stealers in the game. He helped the Dodgers win the pennant in 1947, 1949, 1952, 1953, 1955, and 1956. In 1955, they won the World Series for the first time.

Jackie retired in 1956 at the age of thirty-eight. He was elected to the Baseball Hall of Fame in January, 1962, on the very first vote. Jackie became active in civil rights issues and wrote a sports and civil rights column for *The New York Post*. He suffered a heart attack and died at his home in Connecticut on October 24, 1974. He was only fifty-three. Thousands of people attended Jackie's funeral, and millions mourned the loss of one of the greatest players in baseball history.

Accomplishments

1939 Graduated from Pasadena Junior College, attended UCLA.

1945 Joined the Kansas City Monarchs baseball team of the Negro Leagues.

1947 Signed with the Brooklyn Dodgers.

1949 Named Most Valuable Player in the National League.

1962 Elected into the Baseball Hall of Fame.

Wilma Rudolph

In 1944, when she was four years old, she came down with polio and lost the use of her left leg.

I t is difficult for anyone to become an Olympic athlete, but for Wilma it was a miracle. In 1944, when she was four years old, she came down with polio and lost the use of her left leg. It seemed as if she might have to spend the rest of her life in a leg brace or even a wheelchair.

But Wilma and her family were determined that she would overcome her polio. The doctors suggested massage to strengthen Wilma's muscles, and many times each day her older brothers and sisters took turns massaging her leg. Wilma also practiced walking and exercising, sometimes sneaking off her brace and trying to walk without it.

Five years later, in 1949, she stunned her doctors when she took off her brace and walked on her own. Soon she was running and playing basketball with her brothers and sisters.

Wilma desperately wanted to play basketball for her high school team, but she could not convince the coach to let her join. Finally she was accepted because the coach wanted Wilma's older sister to play, and her father agreed only if Wilma could be on the team too.

Wilma became an excellent basketball player and set a state scoring record. Her coach asked her to join the newly formed girls' track team, and Wilma found that she was best in the sprint. When she was thirteen years old, she ran twenty races and won them all. In four seasons of high school track meets, she never lost a race.

In 1956, at the age of sixteen, she qualified for the Olympic games in Melbourne, Australia. She came home with a bronze medal, determined that one day she would win a gold.

Personality Profile

Career: Track-and-field athlete.

Born: June 23, 1940, in St. Bethlehem, Tennessee, to Ed and Blanche Rudolph.

Died: November 24, 1994, in Nashville, Tennessee.

Education: Tennessee State University, B.A., 1963.

Awards: Won three Olympic gold medals, 1960; James E. Sullivan Memorial trophy, Female Athlete of the Year, 1961; member of U.S. Olympic Hall of Fame and National Track and Field Hall of Fame.

Wilma entered Tennessee State University in 1958, studying elementary education. In those days athletic scholarships were less common than now, and Wilma had to work two hours each day at odd jobs on the university campus to pay her fees. She spent all her spare time training, and by 1960 she was ready to go to the Summer Olympics in Rome, Italy. Wilma won three gold medals and set a new world record in the 100-meter sprint.

After her win, Wilma became an instant star. Crowds gathered wherever she ran, she was honored by parades, appeared on television, and was invited to the White House by President Kennedy. Wilma made a decision not to enter the 1964 Olympic games because she felt she might not do so well this time. She retired from amateur athletics in 1963.

Wilma finished her university degree and became a school teacher and track coach at the same school she had attended as a child. Later she started her own organization to help amateur athletes and to run inner-city sports clinics. Wilma died of brain cancer at her home in Nashville, Tennessee, in 1994.

Accomplishments

1956 Won an Olympic bronze medal in the relay.	**1961** Received the James E. Sullivan Memorial trophy as the country's best amateur athlete.
1960 Won three Olympic gold medals. Tied the world record in the 100-meter and set a new Olympic record in the 200.	**1977** Published her autobiography, *Wilma*. It was made into a television movie.

Index

1 2 3 4 5 6 7 8 9 0 Printed in Canada 4 3 2 1 0 9 8 7 6 5